The Terracotta Army: The History of Ancient China's Famous Terracotta Warriors and Horses

By Charles River Editors

A picture showing some of the sculptures in Pit 1

About Charles River Editors

Charles River Editors provides superior editing and original writing services across the digital publishing industry, with the expertise to create digital content for publishers across a vast range of subject matter. In addition to providing original digital content for third party publishers, we also republish civilization's greatest literary works, bringing them to new generations of readers via ebooks.

Sign up here to receive updates about free books as we publish them, and visit Our Kindle Author Page to browse today's free promotions and our most recently published Kindle titles.

Introduction

A picture of Pit 1

The Terracotta Army

"The terracotta army was a one-off creation, original in both concept and execution, unmentioned in any source, no sooner buried than destroyed and forgotten. ... Why so realistic? Why this many? Why full-size? Why clay? ... The initial inspiration was the need to duplicate a new force, of which the main element was infantry, conscripted from the emperor's newly acquired masses of peasants, and protected not with custom-made armor but with scales of leather and simple, standardized weapons. It was the combination of archers, infantry and charioteers, this particular balance between officers and men, that had enabled the First Emperor to unify the nation." - John Man, *The Terracotta Army: China's First Emperor and the Birth of a Nation*

China has always fascinated outsiders, much in the same way that distant light fascinates someone looking down a dark road. It is both familiar and mysterious, ancient and new, and fully understanding it seems to always remain just out of reach. From the Great Wall to the ancient teachings of Confucius, China's natural and man-made wonders have been topics of interest among Westerners since the Middle Ages and the pursuit of trade routes both by land

and sea, amazing Marco Polo and 19th century British expeditions in similar ways despite the passage of several centuries between them.

For these reasons, it comes as little surprise that people across the world were excited when it was revealed in 1974 that archaeologists had uncovered a new and amazing find: an underground army consisting of thousands of clay soldiers, still standing at their posts despite being over 2,000 years old. In addition to the remarkable feats of craftsmanship and the almost unimaginable size and scale of the Terracotta Army, the sculpted statues seemed to bear testimony of something that modern people could not quite wrap their minds around, representing a time when China was born almost 200 years before Christ. The hope for many was that this remarkable army could reveal the secrets of China's first emperor, Qin Shi Huang, a man who united seven warring tribes into one of the most powerful nations on earth.

Even as research continues 40 years after the initial find, some of the facts about the Terracotta Army are staggering. It's estimated that the army consists of 8,000 soldiers, 130 chariots, and hundreds of horses and cavalry, all of which were sculpted on a mass scale by various factories but were subsequently molded to feature their own unique appearances separate of one another. As if that wasn't enough, there are also terracotta sculptures of acrobats, servants, and musicians, and the sculptures were painted (though most of the paint has faded away over time). This impressive horde of funerary art was buried with Qin Shi Huang to serve him in the afterlife, much the same way Egyptian pyramids were constructed for pharaohs.

While the sculptures comprising the Terracotta Army are impressive as a work of art, they have indeed proven to be an invaluable historical source as well. Thanks to collections of weapons buried with the sculptures, as well as the shapes and sizes of the various military equipment, historians can get a sense of what Qin Shi Huang had at his disposal when he fought battles, and the Terracotta Army itself is even organized based on military rank, allowing historians a chance to understand ancient Chinese military formations.

The Terracotta Army: The History of Ancient China's Famous Terracotta Warriors and Horses chronicles the history of the Chinese emperor who commissioned them and a description of the famous funerary art. Along with pictures of important people, places, and events, you will learn about the Terracotta Army like never before, in no time at all.

The Terracotta Army: The History of Ancient China's Famous Terracotta Warriors and Horses
About Charles River Editors
Introduction

Chapter 1: The Life of the Emperor
Chapter 2: Preparing for Death
Chapter 3: Designing the Army
Chapter 4: Creating the Army
Chapter 5: Painting the Army
Chapter 6: Losing the Army
Chapter 7: Finding the Army
Chapter 8: Studying and Preserving the Army
Bibliography

Chapter 1: The Life of the Emperor

Peter Morgan's picture of two Terracotta sculptures

"Power made the First Emperor a terrifying figure. He seems to have been physically unattractive - high pointed nose, slit eyes, pigeon breast, stingy, cringing, graceless. Traditional portraits of him don't conform to this lean and hungry image, showing him as bearded, bulky, and always wearing headgear like a mortarboard with tassels dangling down the front to hide his semi-divine features from mortal gaze. It's all totally inauthentic, of course, since there were no contemporary portraits; but as with Christ, Genghis Khan and alien abductors, there arose an accepted, iconic version of what he was supposed to look like. Certainly he was moody, easily angered, unpredictable: traits that he shared with other dictators (Hitler and Stalin come to mind). Almost from his own day, the First Emperor was seen as a 'brutal tyrant, inhumanely impressing hundreds of thousands of people into forced labor to fulfil his grandiose ambitions'. It has been part of accepted history that he burned books, destroyed the records of his predecessors and buried scholars alive because they opposed him. His ruthlessness has been a fact of life for the past two millennia. National unity was bought with extreme suffering, was it not?" – John Man, *The Terracotta Army: China's First Emperor and the Birth of a Nation*

Before the famous Terracotta Army could be discovered in the late 20th century, they had to be created, and that was the work of Qin Shi Huang (260-210 BCE), now considered the first Emperor of China. All great men are subject throughout the centuries to the vagaries of public opinion, and Qin Shi Huang was no different. During the centuries following his death, he has been described as everything from a genius to a fool, and from a divine leader of a needy people to a ruthless tyrant. While it is far too late for anyone to know the full truth, chances are that he was a little bit of all these, neither an angel nor a demon but merely a man who had great power and great responsibilities. Part of the problem in trying to understand Qin Shi Huang lies in the fact that his successor hated him and therefore insisted that the records of his reign cast him in the worst possible light. Therefore, the fact that he united the nation was overshadowed in his biographies by an emphasis on how ruthless he had to be, or chose to be, in order to accomplish that feat.

A depiction of Qin Shi Huang

A modern statue of Qin Shi Huang located near the Terracotta Army

Technically, there were other emperors before Qin Shi Huang, but they were less powerful men who ruled small kingdoms around Central Asia. In fact, when Qin Shi Huang was born in 260 BCE and named Zheng, his father's kingdom of Qin was at war with all six of the other small kingdoms. Likewise, when King Zheng ascended the throne at the age of 13, he inherited a kingdom long at war and full of scandal. According to the ancient Chinese historian Sima Qian, "Three years after he ascended the throne King Zhuangxiang passed away and Crown Prince Zheng was set up as king. He honored Lü Buwei by making him chief minister, and entitled him 'uncle'. Since the King of Qin was young, the Queen Dowager from time to time had illicit relations in secret with Lü Buwei. And Buwei had a myriad household servants. … In the ninth year of the First Emperor there was a report that Lao Ai [a member of the queen's household] … had plotted with the Queen Dowager, saying: 'Once the King passes away, we will make our son succeed.' At that the King of Qin handed him over to the law officers for trial and, when all the facts had been obtained, Chief Minister Lü Buwei was implicated in the affair. In the ninth month Lao Ai was wiped out with all his kinsmen, and the two children born of the Queen Dowager were put to death, and then the Queen Dowager was removed to Yong."

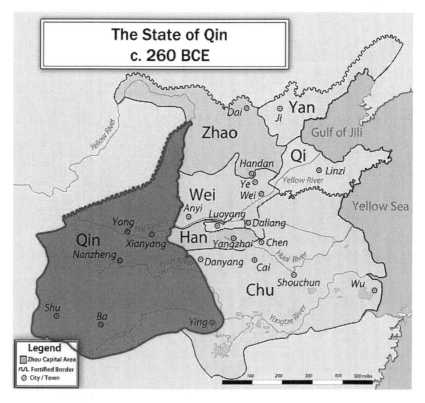

A map of ancient China at the time of Qin Shi Huang's birth

With his throne secure, Qin Shi Huang was able to focus his attention on defeating the other six rivals. The seven empires had been at war with each other for more than 250 years, but he intended to bring that war to an end by decisively winning it. According to Sima, "When the men of Qin opened the pass and engaged the enemy, the armies of the nine states fled and did not dare advance. Without Qin incurring the expenditure of losing a single arrow, all under Heaven had certainly been thrown into difficulties. Thereupon the north–south alliance broke up and its agreements were nullified, and the states vied with each other to bribe Qin by ceding territory. With its surplus strength, Qin was in control of their demise. They pursued the fleeing and drove them northwards, slaughtering the millions so that their shields floated on a sea of blood. Taking advantage of the situation, Qin annexed all under Heaven and split up the mountains and rivers so that the strong states begged to offer their submission and the weak states came to pay homage."

He first conquered Han, then Zhao, and then Wei, Chu, and Yan before finally subduing Qi in 221. With that, Qin had unified the kingdoms under the name of China (*Zhongguo* or "Middle Kingdom"), As a result, though he was not yet 40 years old, Qin Shi Huang was the most powerful man in Asia. Naturally, he intended to stay that way, and he changed his title from King Zheng (of Qin) to Emperor Qin Shi Haung, ruler of a united China. Sima wrote, "When the First Emperor of Qin, having unified all under Heaven, had become emperor, someone said: 'The Yellow Emperor obtained the Power of Earth, and a yellow dragon and an earthworm appeared. The Xia obtained the Power of Wood, and a green dragon stopped at the bounds, and the grass and trees became luxuriant. The Yin obtained the Power of Metal, and silver flowed forth from the mountains. The Zhou obtained the Power of Fire, and there was the omen of the red bird. Now that the Qin has replaced the Zhou, it is time for the Power of Water. ... Thereupon Qin renamed the Yellow River as the 'Powerful Water', and took the tenth month, which was in winter, as the beginning of the year."

Qin Shi Huang also made other changes, as Sima observed. While many of them may seem arbitrary to modern readers, the emperor likely saw them as a necessary part of nation building, and a way of encouraging those he had conquered to let go of their individual pasts and unite. Sima explained, "Among colors they gave priority to black, and they treated six as the basis for measurement, and in sounds they gave priority to dalü, and in the conduct of affairs they gave priority to law. Three years after he had assumed the position of emperor, he journeyed east and toured the provinces and districts. He made a sacrifice at Mount Yi in Zou and extolled the exploits of Qin."

While it was no doubt difficult to teach people to count in a different way or to worship in a new manner, what ultimately proved too difficult for him was working with the followers of Confucius, who was still revered as an inspired spiritual leader despite being long dead. Sima noted, "He then summoned seventy Confucian masters and scholars of broad learning from Qi and Lu who were in attendance to come to the foot of Mount Tai. Among the various Confucian masters someone counselled that 'When the feng and shan were performed in antiquity, the carriage wheels were wrapped in rushes, for they hated to do harm to the soil or vegetation on the mountain; they sacrificed when the earth had been swept, and for mats they used rushes and grain-stalks, so the description would be easy to comply with.' The First Emperor heard the counsel of these people, but each suggestion was bizarre and difficult to adopt, and as a result he got rid of the Confucian masters."

An ancient portrait depicting Confucius

Ultimately, nothing secures a leader's future like pleasing his people, and with that in mind, Qin Shi Huang began a number of public works projects designed to improve transportation and make it easier for the citizens to worship as he wanted them to. Sima wrote, "Next he opened up a roadway for carriages and, ascending via the southern face of Mount Tai, he reached the summit, where a stone tablet was set up, extolling the virtue of the First Emperor of Qin, to make clear that he had been able to perform the feng sacrifice. He descended via a route on the northern side of the mountain, and made the shan sacrifice at Liangfu. In the ceremonies for this they drew to some extent on the procedures which had been used by the Great Supplicator when he sacrificed to the Supreme God at Yong. But the feng sacrifice was hidden away and kept totally secret so that it could not be recorded by contemporaries."

Chapter 2: Preparing for Death

"We don't know much about the afterlife, but we assume a general principle: as below, so above. The spirit world was ruled like a Chinese kingdom, under the direction of the Yellow Emperor, one of the mythical five founder-emperors, with teams of messengers and powers and bureaucrats who kept tabs on the lives and deaths of individuals. In attendance were the spirits of ancestors, who were joined by the newly dead, forming a sort of community of the spirits. It was this belief in a 'spirit community' that injected into China a deep concern with the afterlife; a concern, an obsession, as powerful and as thoroughly human as that of almost any other culture you care to mention. No one except a few skeptical philosophers doubted that there was a hidden reality, the world of the dead, and that there were deep patterns connecting that world, with its various guides and entities - gods, forces, ancestral spirits - to this one. There was, however, much uncertainty about the nature of that connection, how to make contact with the spirit world, and how best to deal honorably with it or control it. In temples devoted to the ancestors, priests did their best with rituals, sacrifices and offerings, which would draw ancestral spirits down from the sphere of the highest god, Shang Di, as he or it was named. Oracles revealed the spirits' will to the living." – John Man, *The Terracotta Army: China's First Emperor and the Birth of a Nation*

For better or worse, most of the changes that Qin Shi Huang made in China would die with him, but he did create two things that would fulfill his dream of being remembered forever. As the seven individual states vied for supremacy over each other through constant warfare, northern barbarians were also a constant menace. Eventually, the Chinese succeeded in eliminating many of those on their immediate northern border, but it was a bittersweet victory because it meant there was no longer a buffer between China and the even fiercer Mongols further north.[1] This new proximity led to increased cultural exchange, as well as the Chinese adoption of nomadic fighting techniques.[2]

Ultimately, it was the wall of the state of Qin that was the first to earn the name great (literally: long) wall,[3] because the state of Qin proved most adept at the new warfare and conquered all the others under Qin Shi Huang. The emperor used the previous walls as the foundation for a new wall. Connecting, rebuilding, and expanding these under harsh rule, the state of Qin demarcated its northern boundary with a longer long wall. According to Sima, "After Qin had unified the world Meng Tian was sent to command a host of three hundred thousand to drive out the Rong and Di along the north. He took from them the territory to the south of the [Yellow] River, and built a Long Wall constructing its defiles and passes in accordance with the configuration of the terrain. It started at Lintao, and extended to Liaodong, reaching a distance of more than ten thousand *li*."[4]

---

[1] Lovell, 39.
[2] Lovell, 40.
[3] Li Feng ch. 9.

The wall spanned about 3,000 kilometers (1,800 miles) and would have required tremendous manpower to build, even with the many gaps in the line and the inconsistencies that resulted from the various landscapes.[5] One official in the subsequent Han Dynasty described the land upon which the Qin wall was built: "[T]he land was brackish and arid, crops could not be grown on them. [...] At the time, the young men being drafted were forced to haul boats and barges loaded with baggage trains upstream to sustain a steady supply of food and fodder to the front. Starting out from the east at the counties of Huang and Hou; and Langye Prefecture the supply lines extended for a tremendous distance to the Beihe River. Commencing at the departure point a man and his animal could carry thirty zhong (~176 kilograms (388 lb)) of food supply, by the time they arrived at the destination, they merely delivered one dan (~29 kilograms (64 lb)) of supply…When the populace had become tired and weary they started to dissipate and abscond. The orphans, the frail, the widowed and the seniors were desperately trying to escape from their appallingly derelict state and died on the wayside as they wandered away from their home. People started to revolt."

A section of the Great Wall of Qin in Jinan

---

[4] Sima Qian in Lovell, 54.
[5] Lindesay, 21. Lovell, 43.

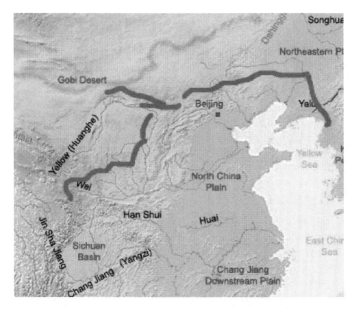

Outline of the walls constructed during the Qin Dynasty

Although the Great Wall of China is one of the world's most famous landmarks today, Qin Shi Huang and his dynasty ruled with such harshness that contemporaries viewed the construction of the wall not only as a source of resentment for the Qin people but even a critical factor in the fall of the dynasty.[6] Put simply, Qin Shi Huang and his people had created a war machine; in addition to defeating the Mongols north of the border and expanding their control there, the Qin dynasty also fought expansionary wars in all directions. Indeed, many of the walls appear so far away from previously settled territory that their purpose appears to have been offensive rather than defensive.[7]

Qin Shi Huang's other project was of a more personal nature. With his power on earth secured, he began to think about his immortality, and how to rule in the next world as he had in this one. Unlike his predecessors, he believed he was immortal and descended not from an earthly father but from the ancient Sage Kings, godlike men who were said to have ruled China in a prehistoric time long ago. Thus, he assumed that he would go on ruling after his death, and in that case, he would have to continue to build the kingdom he had created.

Qin Shi Huang was not unique among ancient rulers when it came to such thoughts, as many

---

[6] Li Feng ch. 11.
[7] Lovell, 43.

other civilizations had very elaborate burial rituals, especially for rulers. The most famous of these rituals concerned the burials of the Egyptian pharaohs, but the Chinese rulers were just as interested in a proper afterlife. In fact, according Sima Qian, Qin Shi Huang wasted no time in planning his own funeral, beginning while he was still a very young man. "When the First Emperor first came to the throne, the digging and preparation work began at Mount Li. Later, when he had unified his empire, 700,000 men were sent there from all over his empire. They dug through three layers of groundwater, and poured in bronze for the outer coffin. Palaces and scenic towers for a hundred officials were constructed, and the tomb was filled with rare artifacts and wonderful treasure. Craftsmen were ordered to make crossbows and arrows primed to shoot at anyone who enters the tomb. Mercury was used to simulate the hundred rivers, the Yangtze and Yellow River, and the great sea, and set to flow mechanically. Above were representation of the heavenly constellations, below, the features of the land. Candles were made from fat of 'man-fish', which is calculated to burn and not extinguish for a long time."

Ironically, Sima Qian never mentioned what would become the most interesting feature of the tomb, the huge Terracotta Army built to accompany the emperor to his grave and serve him in the afterlife. This might be because the idea of using an army made of clay was a somewhat new idea; traditionally, great leaders had been accompanied into the afterlife by court members and soldiers who were simultaneously sacrificed and buried along with their leader. Indeed, other Chinese rulers had done that. Jing Hiongwei, one of the men who worked on unearthing and preserving the Terracotta Army, explained, "When Qin Jing Gong passed away, he buried 186 living people with him. ... They were buried in these coffins. Each coffin was numbered, and each victim was also given a number. Every victim was buried in the coffin with his or her number. The position of every coffin had been pre-assigned. ... Almost every big tomb would have 100 to 200 corpses. This is a massive number. ... Some people were terrified and unwilling to die. But some other people thought their lives were meaningless without their master, so they wanted to follow their master to death, and considered this as a big honor. ... We tested the chemical composition of the skull and hair and found that they both contained arsenic. ... Arsenic can be dissolved in alcohol. So we think that these victims drank arsenic wine and were poisoned to death."

In the same vein, Chinese historian Zhang Zhongli pointed out, "At that time, people believed that there was another world where people could carry on their lives after death ... Rulers' attendants and followers were enjoying their lives with their masters when he was alive. So it was quite natural to follow him when he died ... For them, death was another form of life. ... In a tomb about three hundred years older than the first emperor, we found small pottery figurines some tens of centimeters high. This shows that pottery figurines were replacing living beings as burial objects. From that point on, tombs which we found had more and more stuff of this kind. ... In a tomb about three hundred years older than the first emperor, we found small pottery figurines some tens of centimeters high. This shows that pottery figurines were replacing living beings as burial objects."

It's possible that the terracotta sculptures were ultimately designed to avoid having to sacrifice the living. After all, had Qin Shi Huang believed that being surrounded by the bodies of his murdered retainers was the appropriate thing to do, he would not have hesitated to order it. However, it seems that by the time of his reign, attitudes had changed. Guo Xingwen, who also worked on the Terracotta Army, explained, "Today, we regard this as an inhumane thing. In ancient times, it was considered inhumane as well. Most of the court officials weren't willing to die. But they didn't have any choice, since they would have been disloyal if they didn't. The ritual system required them to die ... It would be their honor to follow the monarch, despite the fact that none of them would really like it. ... At that time human life became more important ... As a consequence of years of war, the population had decreased significantly. Each state was struggling to maintain its population, since population means productivity."

As Guo pointed out, there were no longer enough strong soldiers in China to kill off large numbers of people just to satisfy the vanity of a dying ruler, even one as powerful as Qin Shi Huang. Furthermore, it couldn't have been lost on a man who forged his empire through military means that sacrificing people at his death meant they wouldn't be around to fight to preserve what he had already worked so hard to create.

There were probably other factors influencing Qin Shi Huang's decision as well. Historian Lukas Nickel notes that around this time, the people of Asia were traveling further and further away from their home countries and were thus encountering new ideas and ways of doing things. Nickel noted, "Sculpture as an artistic medium was widely employed in the arts of Greece and the Hellenistic East, but played only a minor role in ancient East Asia. This changed dramatically with the First Emperor of China who marked his ascent to the throne in 221 BC with the erection of giant bronze sculptures outside his palace and the installation of thousands of terracotta figures in his tomb. [There was a] sudden and short-lived surge of sculpture making in third-century BC China...in the context of developments across Asia of the time. [There is] art historical, archaeological and textual evidence to [indicate that] the First Emperor's extraordinary interest in sculpture may have been the result of contacts with the contemporary Hellenistic world."

Obviously, Dr. Nickel's theory attracted significant attention among those working on the Terracotta Army, and he was questioned about his work. In one interview, he observed, "The thousands of terracotta sculptures found in the tomb of the First Emperor have no obvious predecessors in Chinese art history. One has to ask where the concept for this new art medium originated. Archaeology has shown that sculpture was widely employed in Hellenistic Bactria at the time, and references in Chinese literature now suggest that the idea came from there."

However he came upon his decision, it's apparent that Qin Shi Huang still thought he would need a staff and army in the afterlife. While it would be easy to bury the necessary objects, finding people was a different story, and since he was hesitant to sacrifice the living, he ultimately figured he would need to replace them somehow. Ultimately, they came in the form of clay figures of men, women and animals that would be entombed with him, and befitting a man of his stature, the clay figures would be properly life-sized so they would be large enough to use the items included in the tomb. Furthermore, each figure would be unique, just as each of his subjects was unique.

Picture of a soldier and horse

A picture of soldiers that indicates their unique features

Putting all of these thoughts together, Qin Shi Huang fashioned his greatest project: the creation of a fully outfitted and equipped army of clay. To accomplish this, the emperor created a two-pronged plan, one to expand his kingdom on earth and the other to further his ambitions in the afterlife. According to Sima, "Coming to the time when the First Emperor of Qin unified all under Heaven, when he reached the sea coast innumerable magicians mentioned [new] places. The First Emperor considered going to sea himself, but was afraid he would not reach them, so he appointed someone to send youths and maidens to sea in search of them. Although boats passed backwards and forwards over the sea, they all made the wind their excuse and said that they had so far been unable to get there, but had seen them in the distance. Next year the First Emperor again travelled along the sea coast, and went as far as Langye. He passed Mount Heng and returned via Shangdang. Three years later he travelled to Jieshi and interrogated the magicians who had gone to sea, and then returned home via Shang province. Five years later the First Emperor went south and reached Mount Xiang, and next he climbed Kuaiji and went along the sea coast, hoping to come across the marvelous elixirs from the three spirit mountains in the sea. He did not obtain them and, when he reached Shaqiu on his return, he passed away."

Chapter 3: Designing the Army

The mound that serves as the location of the emperor's tomb

"Since the next life was thought to reflect this one, and since soldiers would anyway be part of life in the tomb, unity would have to be achieved and/or maintained in the afterlife as well. Unification and the army would be honored together. To reflect the novelty of what had been achieved by the emperor and his army, a new level of realism was called for. How better to achieve this than by giving the spirit army real weapons, which already existed by the ten thousand and which could be topped up by long-established manufacturing techniques? And if the weapons were real, clearly they could not be held by anything but full-size figures." – John Man, *The Terracotta Army: China's First Emperor and the Birth of a Nation*

If there was one thing that Qin Shi Huang knew how to design and organize, it was an army. After all, it was he who managed to win a war that had been raging for more than 250 years, and he defeated not one but six rivals, so he had a fairly good idea of the size and scope of an army that he would need to fight his battles in the afterlife. His army would have to be big, preferably at least 10,000 thousand strong (though to date only 8,000 clay soldiers have been uncovered), and it would also have to be orderly, for he did not want to have to worry about squabbling forces. As such, there would have to be a hierarchy, and a chain of command that would provide proper leadership. With that in mind, there had to be officers among the thousands of warriors who could give orders and plan battles for the rest.

Given that he had won several campaigns, it's no surprise that Qin Shi Huang figured he would need specialized divisions. It would not be good enough to merely have an entire army consisting of infantry depending on terrain, so he needed archers and horsemen to complement them, and if the Terracotta Army was going to include cavalry, clay horses would be necessary too.

Picture of a terracotta archer

Picture of horses included among the Terracotta Army

As for where to build his army, Qin Shi Huang already had a perfect location in mind because he had already had men working on his tomb since he won his final battles for unification. In all, the emperor ordered four giant pits dug to house his body and his mighty eternal army, but of course, that was easy work compared to the tasks facing the craftsmen who would have to create thousands of unique warriors, each standing around six feet tall and weighing in excess of 600 pounds. As Chinese historian Zhang Zhongli himself learned, "Human-size statues are definitely harder than small statues to make. Whoever came up with the idea might not have known how difficult making them was going to be. … We started to make 40cm, 50cm, and finally…one half of human size, about 1 meter tall."

A group of soldiers in Pit 1

As a result, the process of creating the Terracotta Army would require the best and brightest minds in unified China, which actually proved to be beneficial in that it united people toward a common goal. Workers who might otherwise not have been able to earn a living were put to work on the project and paid a salary out of the emperor's own treasury, and since each soldier was unique, the people working on them had a chance to feel that they were contributing to something that would exist long after they had died as well.

Furthermore, the emperor's exacting standards, while making the task far more complex, also motivated workers who were responsible for the quality and quantity of their own work in various ways. Indeed, when the terracotta soldiers were uncovered, researchers found that the sculptures were marked in ways that would identify who had worked on them. As archaeologist Yuan Zhongyi explained, "In each of the figurines you can find the name of the craftsperson in the most hidden places. They did this in hope that people wouldn't see their names. This is to allow their managers and superiors to check their work. If things are not constructed well, the worker may be asked to re-craft them or, in the worst case scenario, go to jail or be decapitated."

As exciting and attractive as the project was, it was also daunting and intimidating. Each soldier would require many hours of labor to produce, and each horse required even more. Furthermore, before any artisan could begin his work, unskilled laborers would have to dig tons of clay from the ground. The project would require every worker to do their utmost, even though the work was intended to be sealed into a tomb with the emperor and thus hidden forever. Some might think that the fact that the Terracotta Army was meant to be buried for eternity would take the pressure for perfection off, but the emperor believed that nothing but perfection would do. With that, everything from the hair on their heads to the nails on their toes had to be perfectly crafted, and likewise, all the clothing and items that each soldier carried had to be perfect, including his weapons, shoes, armor and armbands.

Despite the requirements, the project eventually began with shovels being pushed into the clay beds near China's rivers. It would take decades to complete and millennia to be fully appreciated, but it would certainly succeed in the goal of making Emperor Qin Shi Huang immortal, at least in the minds of those who ever got to see or read about the Terracotta Army.

Chapter 4: Creating the Army

Pictures of rows and columns of soldiers

"Other considerations were cost and speed of manufacture. No point in an ambition that could not be realized in something like the time it would take to build the tomb - a few years. And no point either in decreeing full-size figures made in bronze, say, or jade, let alone gold. Even in bronze, several thousand full-size figures would stretch the Qin budget beyond breaking point, even if the expert artisans could be gathered. The figures could conceivably have been made of wood. But the labour of carving each figure would have been immense. What was required was a way of mass-producing the figures, fast. That left only one possible medium: clay. All of China's diverse cultures understood clay. There were and are beds of it all over north China, so it was cheap, widely available and easily worked. Moreover, clay had been used in mass production techniques for well over 1,000 years." – John Man, *The Terracotta Army: China's First Emperor and the Birth of a Nation*

While it might now seem to have been a foregone conclusion to use clay when constructing the Terracotta Army, there were other options to consider for the emperor and his workers. For instance, the statues could have been made of metal, as many items at that time were cast of bronze or made of beaten iron, but this was likely ruled out due to exorbitant costs and the fact that coming up with enough metal for as many as 10,000 soldiers would have taken decades. Also, it would have been very difficult to shape metal into realistically lifelike shapes. Wood, on the other hand, was plentiful and easy to carve, but it was common knowledge that the wood decayed quickly, rotting away in a matter of years if not carefully preserved. Therefore, wood was not an ideal option either.

That left clay, a substance that had been used for centuries to create everything from gods to chamber pots, but even this decision had to be refined, because not just any clay would do. It had to be thick and sticky enough to stay in one piece as it dried out, but not so sticky that it would not dry at all. Fortunately for planners, the clay pits around the tomb site proved to be just the substance for the job, and that was where the story of the Terracotta Army's construction would begin. With thousands of years of water leaving behind huge streaks of heavy red clay, China was home to some of the finest clay in the world, as Zhang Zhongli, himself an artist who made a living by recreating statues from the Terracotta Army to sell to tourists and collectors, explained, "This is called red clay, it is sticky and strong. We searched many places and could not find anywhere else with this much red clay. But we find that this place has a lot. Now we only use red clay from here to make terracotta warriors. 2000 years ago, I think Terracotta Warriors were impossible to be made with other soil or clay."

While the diggers were beginning to wrest heavy clay from the resistant ground, the artisans commissioned to create the army got to work planning how they would go about their task. The big question was how to make so many warriors quickly enough to be ready for burial by the end of the emperor's lifetime. He was already nearly 40 years old when the project began, and life expectancy in ancient China was not nearly as long as it is today. Also, the Emperor was ruling over a united but volatile empire full of people who had been at war with each other for centuries before he established peace through victory, so there was always the possibility that he could be assassinated or killed in battle, which made the task even more urgent.

At first, the workers considered creating molds that could be altered slightly for each soldier in order to make each figure unique, but molded statues would almost certainly have to be solid and would thus weigh more than 1,000 pounds each, an unmanageable situation. As an alternative, they considered other methods of construction before finally settling on one as old as the first clay bowl and as new as a child's first time playing with a malleable substance: creating long ropes of clay and coiling them to create a rough outline of each body before going back and adding unique details later.

While this was probably the best option given the circumstances, it was hardly an easy one to manage. As Zhang noted, "The ancient craftsmen used a simple method; they pounded the clay until it became soft, and rolled the clay into strips. Then they coiled the clay strips upward, we call this method clay-coiling ...the first emperor's craftsmen were the first people in China to make statues this way." Han Ping Zhe, who worked for a company that produced copies of terracotta warriors to sell, described the process in more detail, based on his own study of some broken soldiers: "This...broken half body gives us very important information about how terracotta warriors were made. We can see the internal traces of the clay layers here, which shows how the clay coiled up. The sign of how the clay coiled up and joined together is very clear. Here is one clay coil, here is another clay coil. One coil after another, until the clay layers were all joined up inside the body. You see this layer, this layer, this layer and this layer ... Until it reaches this place, near the bottom, one by one ... So, this is how a terracotta warrior is made."

Pictures of broken soldiers

Lest this method call to mind a vision of a kindergartener making a small bowl for their parents, it's important to remember that these coiled soldiers were around six feet tall but with body walls that were only half an inch thick. As anyone who has ever tried to coil the sides of a pot knows, there is a limit to how high one can go before the weight of the coils cause the walls to collapse. As Mao Sanxue, a master craftsman who today constructs copies of the warriors using traditional methods, observed, "When I looked at the terracotta warriors, I was amazed by the ancient people's achievement. My statues collapsed 3 or 4 times when I first started." To overcome this problem, the artists worked on each soldier a few inches at a time, allowing the clay to dry and harden between sessions, but even this was a tense process because each soldier had to be completed before the first clay used became so dry that it cracked. Archaeologist Neil Harrison shared Mao's amazement, saying, "Well when I first saw this I was just in disbelief. It was a big surprise, I mean it was a totally new type of discovery."

Another problem that the laborers faced was dealing with the fluctuating temperatures in northern China, where the winters are frigidly cold and the summers are sweltering. After much research, Zhang has concluded that this problem forced the artisans to dig caves into the sides of nearby mountains, and once inside these well-insulated rooms, they were able to work throughout the year, more or less oblivious to outside temperatures. He explained, "From long experience, I think the coiling method that was used 2000 years ago could not have been done at such temperatures. Ideally the temperature needs to be maintained at around 20 degrees Celsius. … In the summer, the temperature outside may reach 30 Celsius degrees; inside the cave house, it may be only 20-25 Celsius degrees. In the winter, outside maybe-10 Celsius degrees, while the cave-house remains at 15-20 Celsius degrees."

While the bodies were coiled, the features, including the noses, mouths, ears, heads, and hands, were mass produced in molds (though they also received some personal attention before they were fired). Ultimately, however, coiling was the only workable method that could create life-sized sculptures and still meet the emperor's goal of originality. Zhang elaborated on this, saying, "If these statues were made with molding, it would only be efficient if we made the same copy over and over again ... This was not the goal of the ancient people. With the clay-coiling method, it is easier to make each terracotta warrior different, whether it was fat or slim, tall or short ... The idea was to create a group of humans."

Pictures of soldiers in Pit 1

As some workers were working on how to create each warrior, others were busy figuring out how to fire the clay after each was completed, because there was no way that air drying could create the type of hardened figure the emperor demanded. A kiln was needed to harden clay for permanence, but even a very large kiln would be too small for just one of the soldiers being created, much less the multiples that would need to be fired at one time. Khang believes they came up with a clever solution to this problem: "They sculpted the terracotta warriors in cave-houses, then fired the statues after sculpting by sealing the entry of the cave-house and turning it into a kiln, so they could fire the statues inside."

Of course, soldiers are only so useful without good weapons, and a military leader like Qin Shi Huang was understandably determined to equip his army with the best weaponry available. Unlike the warriors, the weapons could be mass-produced and identical, which actually proved to be a big advancement in manufacturing. Archaeologist Yan Fuxing explained, "We found one [crossbow] trigger at one city, and another trigger at another city that is 2000 miles away. Parts of the trigger are exchangeable. In modern terms, these are standardized parts. I don't know how they designed these parts. Even now this is not an easy job, even experienced artisans need to work carefully."

Shashi Bellamkonda's pictures of armor buried with the Terracotta Army

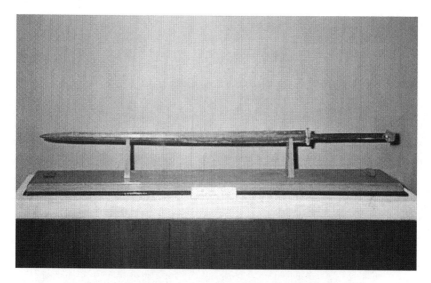

Leon Petrosyan's picture of a sword found in the tomb

In addition to crossbows, archaeologists have found evidence of the arrows fired by them (though the wood and feathers that they were originally made of were gone). Liu Zhangcheng spent years studying the soldiers and their weapons and came to some interesting conclusions: "We found more than 30,000 arrowheads in the pits. We tested the arrowheads, and found the difference in their sizes to be less than 1cm; some of them only have a difference of 0.22mm. The difference is very tiny. We know that weapon manufacturing was standardized. ... Mass production was the only way to explain the large numbers of arrowheads we found ... The difference between arrowheads is tiny. I think they used molds, so they were able to produce massive amounts of arrowheads with tiny differences." Thus, even if the figures needed to be individually created, it's safe to assume that the experience each artisan had with such mass-production techniques still helped move the project along.

Altogether, the process of making the warriors was incredibly complex, and the emperor understood this well enough to assign a large number of craftsmen to work on the project. Researchers have found evidence that at least 87 master craftsmen worked on the Terracotta Army, each with his own team of about 10 assistants. Thus, it's estimated that 11 men worked together to complete about one soldier per month.

Chapter 5: Painting the Army

"Then there are the colors. Color turns out to be a matter of much complexity and labor. It was not shortage of clay or kilns or sculptors, I think, that placed a limit on the number of warriors, but the drive to apply color. For non-specialists, the fact that the warriors were painted is both strange and disturbing, for it flies in the face of the evidence as you see it today. We have all got used to the terracotta warriors looking like terracotta. But they weren't like that at all when they were made. They were lacquered, and bright with reds and blues and greens and purples - not just the uniforms, but the faces too. You have to imagine one of the most famous figures, the towering 'general', as he is known, with painted patterns on his tunic and armor, green and purple clothing, and bright green shin-protectors. And a pink face, like virtually all the warriors: a gentle pink created by mixing red and white, even gentler for the more senior officers, perhaps because (then as now) a pale skin suggested upper-class status, whereas a weather-beaten skin indicated the hard outdoor life of the common soldier." – John Man, *The Terracotta Army: China's First Emperor and the Birth of a Nation*

Pictures of a terracotta soldier with some of the original paint still visible

Pictures of the Terracotta Army are instantly recognizable around the world, and many of them depict rows of solemn, clay-colored statues standing together, but that was not always the case. Fittingly, the same emperor who demanded that each of his solders be unique also required each figure to be painted with colorful pigments created by the best scientists in China. While this strikes some people as strange, it was actually quite normal, according to Catharina Blänsdorf, a German conservator who has worked extensively with the Terracotta Army. She explained, "As so many objects of the antique world were painted - in the West as well as the East - and especially the sculptures, the question should rather be: why not paint them?"

As a result, each soldier received a heavy coat of lacquer, a shiny paint synonymous with

Chinese artifacts for centuries, and there were several reasons why the emperor wanted lacquer to be used. For one thing, it was rare and expensive, which bolstered Qin Shi Huang's status as a wealthy and powerful man, and another reason was that it was shiny, which would make the army stand out. Perhaps most notably, lacquer was tough and was thought to stand the test of time well without fading. Blänsdorf continued, "Lacquer is a very stable material and also in the antiquity they knew that it can survive centuries or even longer. ... So it had technical reasons, but also aesthetically reasons and reasons of meaning. ... Lacquer wares were luxury goods and they probably were so expensive that only the emperor could afford to lacquer a whole army. ... You can't take very much because otherwise the tree will die. So you do it once, let it heal, and then continue."

At the time, lacquer was used on all of China's finest art objects. Produced by the precious lacquer tress, it began as a smelly, syrupy sap that could only be collected during a few short summer months of each year. Even then, the precious lacquer trees did not give up their lifeblood willingly, as only a few tablespoons could be harvested from each tree each year, and if more was taken, the delicate tree would die. Based on these calculations, the sap from 25 different trees would be needed to cover each soldier, more than 2,000 each production year.

Making matters all the more difficult, those who were tasked with lacquering the soldiers were subjected to miserable working conditions, at least in the beginning, because the lacquer tree is a member of the infamous poison ivy family and the precious sap causes a vile, itching reaction anytime it comes in contact with human skin. According to Blänsdorf, "I tried to work with the lacquer several times just to experiments, and in the beginning not much happened, but then twice there was a strong reaction where really my hands and my whole face was covered with this rash. It's not painful. It's just itching and you have to...control yourself a lot not to scratch. And it's not really looking nice. And what normally happens is that you get this reaction several times and then there's an immunization, so afterwards you don't get it anymore."

Though brown in its liquid form, lacquer dried into a clear, hard coat, not unlike modern day clear nail polish. At that point, it became a protective barrier between the paint and the outside world, so it was assumed that at that point, the soldiers would retain the color for eternity. Obviously, this would prove to not be the case. Based on research into the pigment flakes found in the tomb, the lacquer protected beautiful, bright paint jobs featuring all the colors typically found in ancient Chinese art, along with one that was not so typical. Blänsdorf explained, "We're looking at one clump of the Chinese purple pigment and the size is around 50 micron to 50 micron. So it's about...the cross section of your hair...People speculate there is a technology transfer from Egypt to China because of the similarity of those two materials ... Which is really significant in terms of technological development and the communication between two civilizations."

The color, known as "Chinese purple," was one of only two man-made colors known to the ancient world, along with Egyptian blue, which has been found in the tombs of the pharaohs. Even today, scientists have not been able to determine exactly what it is made of. Another thing that makes Chinese purple unique is that it appears to have come out of nowhere and disappeared again just a few hundred years later, as it has not be found on many other surfaces. That said, most people still think it's unlikely that the color came from the Egyptians because there had not yet been any known contact between the two cultures during the 3rd century BCE. As scientist Nobumichi Tamura points out, "It ... [i]ndicates that the Chinese really actually invented the Chinese purple completely independently from the Egyptians; there was no technology transfers at all."

The two substances were made of similar ingredients, with the only difference being that Chinese purple contained barium and Egyptian blue was made with calcium, but Chinese purple contained a substance not used in Egypt: lead oxide. Today, some researchers suspect that Chinese purple had important religious significance, as it was also found on the burial suit of an important Chinese leader.

Chapter 6: Losing the Army

"Let's imagine. Xiang Yu's people had known of the Terracotta Army since 209 BC, when they had been driven off by its hastily recruited laborers. There would have been prisoners, there would have been talk. So in early 206 BC, with the palaces of Xianyang still blazing, Xiang Yu arrives at Lintong, eager for more booty and more vengeance. He knows about the tomb, and also its dangers and difficulties: the risk of mercury poisoning, the loaded crossbows, the depth of soil. He knows, too, of the Terracotta Army, knows that it contains things that would be very useful: not the clay soldiers, of course, but the many thousands of real weapons they hold - the crossbows, bows, swords, lances, dagger-axes, arrows - almost all made of bronze. True, iron would have been better, as several of the Warring States had discovered; but with more fighting to be done, bronze weapons, especially the crossbows with their superb bronze triggers, would be just fine." – John Man, *The Terracotta Army: China's First Emperor and the Birth of a Nation*

There is no way to know how much longer Qin Shi Huang's great project might have gone on had he not died around 210 BCE at the age of 50. Ironically, he lost his life while in pursuit of some sort of "Fountain of Youth" that he had heard could be found in a faraway province. According to Sima, "The First Emperor again travelled along the sea coast, and went as far as Langye. He passed Mount Heng and returned via Shangdang. Three years later he travelled to Jieshi and interrogated the magicians who had gone to sea, and then returned home via Shang province. Five years later the First Emperor went south and reached Mount Xiang, and next he climbed Kuaiji and went along the sea coast, hoping to come across the marvelous elixirs from the three Spirit Mountains in the sea. He did not obtain them and, when he reached Shaqiu on his return, he passed away."

Naturally, the emperor's death necessitated the end of his greatest project, as his burial place was finally put to use to inter his body and his clay army. Tragically, however, his plans to go to the grave only with clay servants was ignored by his successor, Xiang Yu. Instead, according to Sima, "The Second Emperor said: 'It is inappropriate for the wives of the late emperor who have no sons to be free', ordered that they should accompany the dead, and a great many died. After the burial, it was suggested that it would be a serious breach if the craftsmen who constructed the tomb and knew of its treasure were to divulge those secrets. Therefore after the funeral ceremonies had completed, the inner passages and doorways were blocked, and the exit sealed, immediately trapping the workers and craftsmen inside. None could escape. Trees and vegetation were then planted on the tomb mound such that it resembled a hill."

While the tomb was obviously made to look like a hill in order to keep away looters, too many people had seen it being constructed to keep its location a secret, so within just a few years later, it faced the threat of looting. According to the ancient historian Shui Jing Zhu, "Xiang Yu entered the gate, sent forth 300,000 men, but they could not finish carrying away his loot in 30 days. Thieves from northeast melted the coffin and took its copper. A shepherd looking for his lost sheep burned the place, the fire lasted 90 days and could not be extinguished."

Nonetheless, archaeologist Yuan Zhongyi maintains, "There is no evidence of organized destruction. I imagine small groups going to different parts of the same area. But the warriors are close-packed, so it was hard to get through. They were in a rush. We found remains of warriors which seem to have fallen in a zig-zag pattern. This suggests they were pushed over as people forced their way through. One horse was standing apart from its tail, which lay a few meters away, as if someone had thrown it. One of the generals had a broken sword - the top bit, which had gold and jade decorations, had gone, leaving the bottom bit of the blade in its scabbard. And in the hole in Pit Number Two, we found the gold decorations for a horse."

A picture of terracotta soldiers missing the spears they originally held

What is certain is that at some point, a fire broke out in the tomb, badly damaging many of the clay soldiers. Archaeologist Yuan Zhongyi explained, "All the time, I wonder who committed this crime. When we first saw the warriors in Pit Number One, we asked ourselves: who destroyed them? At first some of us said the fire could have been started by natural causes, by spontaneous combustion, from gas. But we could not find any materials that might cause a fire, like straw. Certainly, it could not have started with the warriors. So our second suggestion was that it was the result of a funeral ceremony, a sort of ritual immolation. The Qin burned everything to do with the emperor, perhaps. So I began checking the history books, and realized it must have been to do with Xiang Yu's uprising."

The ancient historian Han Shu seemingly confirmed this theory, writing, "Xiang burned the palaces and buildings. Later observers witnessed the excavated site. Afterward a shepherd lost his sheep which went into the dug tunnel; the shepherd held a torch to look for his sheep, and accidentally set fire to the place and burned the coffin." Still, there were questions over how someone could have done such a thing, and why someone would do such a thing. As Yuan Zhongyi noted, "But where would it start? That hole leading down into Pit Two - there are many ashes around the base. Perhaps what happened is that after robbing the place, the intruders started the fire to stop anyone else coming back for more."

Through the years, different experts have weighed in on the issue, including Joe Lally, an American archaeologist with the Bureau of Land Management in Albuquerque, New Mexico. He explained, "With ventilation being on floor level and none within the upper portions of the compartment, there would be no exit for heat and smoke, which fill a compartment from the top down, no matter where the fire is burning. Heat would not be a problem. Heat loss to the walls (the heat being absorbed) would be more than ten times greater than heat loss through the looters' shaft. The corridors would fill with smoke at the rate of seven cubic metres a second. A medium growth fire would allow 3.8 minutes for a safe exit from anywhere within the structure. The exit time would be increased by creeping low beneath the upper, smoke-filled portions of the corridors."

One of Lally's fellow investigators, Jim Quintière, believed that the fire might not have been started by anyone: "Having investigated several underground woody landfills, which can ignite spontaneously, I believe the earthen-bamboo with moisture-promoting bacterial growth could first produce heat from the bacteria, then chemical heat due to oxidation of the bamboo. This can lead to spontaneous ignition. The nature of the subsequent fire is likely to be smoldering, but can also break out into flames. I have seen this happen. In one fire I know of, the fire moved across the land-fill beneath the ground in days. Later, when the land-fill was covered with asphalt to impede the oxygen flow, temperature soundings still indicated combustion."

Chapter 7: Finding the Army

"In the spring of 1974, the middle of Shaanxi province was stricken by drought. ... One evening in mid-March, the six Yang brothers gathered among the persimmon trees edging the village that bore their family name, Xiyang (West Yang). Squatting on their haunches and smoking, they worried out loud about the lack of water. They all agreed that someone had to do something. They needed water, fast. That meant a new well. ... 'OK, let's make a start,' said one. But where? The most senior of the brothers, Yang Peiyan, looked up at Mount Li, and pointed out a cleft. If there was any water to be had, it would follow that course and feed into the orchards that lay a couple of hundred meters uphill to the south. Nods and grunts of assent: that would be the best spot." – John Man, *The Terracotta Army: China's First Emperor and the Birth of a Nation*

For over 2,000 years, the first emperor's mighty army lay hidden under centuries of mud and sand, silently standing watch just as they were created to do, and during those two millennia, China suffered all kinds of ups and down as dynasties rose and fell until 1912, when a century of unrest gave way to the creation of the Republic of China. The new Chinese government looked with suspicion and disdain on the former one and went out of its way to discourage any praise for China's imperial past. Therefore, when items were found from the era, usually dug up by some rural farmer cultivating a field, they were quickly escorted away and hidden. One Chinese museum executive, Zhao Kangmin, who was given charge of the few items that turned up from time to time, recalled, "They knew I was involved with old things which had something to do with an emperor, so they accused me of encouraging feudalism. Everyone sat, except for me. I was made to stand. They read out a long article listing my mistakes, and told me to admit them. I refused, because I knew everything I had done had been correct. Later I was told to write a letter of apology. Again, I refused. But just to avoid trouble I joined the revolutionary guards until the fuss died down."

Ironically, the great army, made of earth and burned by fire, was ultimately rediscovered because of water. In the years leading up to 1974, certain areas of China suffered a severe drought, forcing people to try to find water by digging new wells, so in March 1974, a group of farming brothers in the Lintong District of Xi'an in the Shaanxi province went out to dig for water. On March 29, after a day or two of backbreaking work, they broke through a particularly hard section into the roof of the buried emperor's mausoleum and discovered huge clay statues of ancient soldiers. Suddenly, the thirst for water became a thirst for knowledge, and understandably, the men who had been digging the well found themselves more interested in the statues than they had originally been in the water. Knowing that what they were seeing was something far beyond their normal purview, they sent word to the local government and asked that someone be sent to properly excavate what they had found.

Given his position and experience, Zhao Kangmin was the one sent out to look at the find. He later wrote, "The first I knew was on April the twenty-eighth, a month after the find, when my bureau chief called me: 'The cadre chief says some farmers have found pottery heads the size of human ones.' I thought: This could be an important discovery. 'Anything else?' I asked. 'Bronze arrowheads. You'd better go and check.' So I got on my bicycle and rode to the field. The Yangs were still at work there, digging their well. I saw seven or eight pieces - bits of legs, arms and two heads - lying near the well, along with some bricks. All the bronze arrowheads had gone.'"

The first people to lay eyes on the figures were in for a big surprise. Catharina Blänsdorf later explained, "Many people were astonished or surprised because they didn't expect them to be so colorful, and some people were also really shocked, because somehow they just liked the terracotta version." When she was able to recreate the paint schemes of some full scale replicas, people continued to be amazed: "And they found it's kind of disturbing and breaking it up. And they really asked me, they asked me, 'are you really sure that it has to be like this?'... It's based on our findings so we're pretty sure that this is true, and they just have to get used to it ... And we tell them that of course we are not going to repaint the originals."

Unfortunately, it soon became apparent that unearthing the figures would permanently change them, because they began to decay quickly after their initial exposure to oxygen. As soon as the lacquer was exposed, it began to dry out very quickly and then flake off, taking the color pigment with it. Blänsdorf noted, "The problem is that the lacquer layer was embedded in the wet soil for 2200 years, And finally the lacquer layers just flake off in tiny flakes and then there's no chance to bring them back to the terracotta. ... We hope that we'll find a method that is simple and cheap, easy to apply during the excavation and that helps preserve the lacquer layers in the first moment. ... When people created the terracotta warriors 2000 years ago, all the pits were full of color ... When we excavated, the paints were almost gone ... Only small areas of paint remained, and those were in poor condition. The paint can easily fall off after excavation."

Going into more detail, Blänsdorf discussed the challenges of preserving the Terracotta Army: "It is a big challenge to preserve and exhibit such a huge excavation in situ. ... Normally, the objects are taken out and are presented in a museum and the site is covered again or destroyed. ... But objects can also be very well preserved in humid or wet environments—for example, on the bottom of the ocean. The material of the object is important. In the given environment in Lintong, inorganic materials such as stone, metal, and pigments are more stable than the organic materials such as wood, fabric, leather, and binding media. This lacquer on the terracotta objects is an organic material. ... What produces the damages are the changes of the environment. If you put objects from dry to wet or wet to dry environment, they 'suffer' from physical and chemical changes taking place. In our case, we have an organic material—the lacquer—that has spent 2,200 years in a wet environment. Water has penetrated into the material, water-soluble components have been 'washed out,' and the whole structure is swollen."

Indeed, the decay takes place so fast upon exposure to oxygen that the color on the statutes completely flakes off before the figures can be transported to a preservation laboratory. Thus, whatever method is designed for preserving the color must be something that can be accomplished in the field, as soon as the item comes out of the ground. Teams of scientists from China and Germany have worked for years on the problem, but success has still managed to elude them. Blänsdorf also discussed their preservation efforts: "After excavation, the water evaporates, the material loses volume, shrinks, and falls apart. ... Without conservation, the paint is completely lost [approximately] 1 week after excavation. ... The loess soil cracks and crumbles, and sensitive organic materials [such] as the poly chromy and remnants of wood, leather, textiles, etc. suffer and decay. With better and more careful methods and treatment of the objects during excavation, much more can be preserved. This is developing in a promising way."

Chapter 8: Studying and Preserving the Army

"It was my first time with a warrior, so I felt a responsibility to remember every touch of the hard, smooth clay. ...I went over the overlapping leather plates of his armor, feeling the rivets and ties, still with traces of red on them, as if I were learning Braille. The right hand was missing, but the left was perfect, down to the well-trimmed fingernails. Fingers that once held the stock of a crossbow rested on a lump of light grey mud that the archer had been pressing against his waist for 2,213 years.... I counted the stipples across and down the non-slip soles of his boots…. I ran my hand over the robe as it swung up over the remarkably solid left thigh. I spotted the maker's signature etched into one of the armor-plates so that his supervisor could hold him to account if need be: his name was Chao or Zhao…and no one had any reason to accuse him of lack of quality. It was a shame the head was missing, but its absence did allow me to feel down inside the neck, where Chao or Zhao's fingers had left their mark as they squeezed the clay into its mold." – John Man, *The Terracotta Army: China's First Emperor and the Birth of a Nation*

In spite of the decaying of the paint on the terracotta warriors, work continued for some time on the excavation, and as of today, the four pits dugs for the entombment have been excavated but only three were found to contain items. It seems that the fourth one was never filled, possibly because Qin Shi Huang's relatively sudden death cut the project short. Thus far, more than 8,000 soldiers have been uncovered, ranging in size and rank from seven foot tall generals to barely six foot tall foot soldiers. There were other terracotta people too, including officials, musicians and other entertainers. There are also 130 authentic chariots with more than 500 life-sized clay horses standing by to pull them, as well as 150 cavalry horses (though most of the latter have not yet been excavated). The tomb housing Qin's body has been located but remains unopened, pending improvements in preservation techniques.

Pictures of two of the Terracotta Army's chariots

Soldiers and horses in Pit 1

Even as preservationists struggle to keep the colors of the Terracotta Army intact, the contents of the pits are still amazing even without their bright colors. Glen Cameron is a facial recognition expert for New Zealand who used a piece of facial recognition software normally used to identify criminals and victims to see what he could learn about the soldiers. He scanned photos of more than 100 warriors before making some startling discoveries: "It's been used throughout Asia and around the world in various forms. In border control, surveillance, immigration, and by the police. We can match around 1 million faces per second. … Let's have a quick look at these top matches here. These two with the big fatter chins. So here we have very similar chin lines with the big thick chin. Similar mouth position. Nose slightly different, but the eyes, eyebrows very different. There is a huge range of faces here. Very individual, very individual. Whole head very different in shape. Facial hair. Very different facial hair. A lot of difference in the eyes. This guy is looking quite sad. Look at the eyebrows on this one. Nearly frowning. Very entertaining facial features in the eyes, in the eyebrows. This one here quite a flat nose. And this one here more normal. There is some similarity between the warriors like some chins, the mouth, the nose. But they are all very unique. I think this is incredibly exciting and I am astounded they could be produced…these sort of numbers and made so, so individual."

Today, the Terracotta Army is big business, as many companies in China have sought to capitalize off their popularity by producing copies of the warriors for collectors around the world. This is somewhat ironic, as Han Ping Zhe, who worked for one of these manufacturing companies, was quick to point out: "Because we mass-produce, making hundreds or thousands copies of one statue, molding is the only way." Han Ping Zhe also described some of the ways the terracotta figures are marketed to individual buyers: "Our Terracotta Warriors are exported to countries like the United State, Germany, Japan, United Kingdom, and France. We manufacture around 50,000 small terracotta warriors each year, and about 200 full-size figures. Besides the traditional statues, we also modify some elements according to our clients' needs. This warrior is playing golf. We made it for our client, the Yajian Golf Club. The golf club gives it to winners as a trophy. … When we opened our business, we weren't sure how to make a terracotta warrior. I read about the traditional clay-coiling method. And we tried it. It took us a month to finish one statue."

Though the methods used are different today, the clay itself is practically the same, a concept that Suchitra Sebastian, another of the men making the modern day soldiers, finds amazing. "It's incredible to think that this material that's been around for more than 2,000 years, that was initially discovered and in fact created by Chinese chemists and has been on this terracotta army for 2,000 years. It's incredible to think that we've re-visited this material, something that's a fundamental advance in our understanding, in our 21th century knowledge of physics. And that's just mind blowing."

Today, the Terracotta Army and all its accoutrements remain housed in a gigantic, state of the art museum built over the burial site. Bigger than a football field, it covers the three excavated pits and, as Blänsdorf has pointed out, is a vital link to China's past. "It is one of the largest burial complexes of Chinese emperors. … The Terracotta Army belongs to the burial complex of the first Chinese emperor, who is very important of Chinese History because he united the China Empire and laid the foundation of the state existing until today. … Later on, the 'normal furnishing' of an emperor's tomb included a Terracotta Army and everything that belonged to the emperor's court. … In the future, with more and more pits unearthed, the focus probably will shift from the terracotta to the mausoleum itself. Slowly we see the army as only a small part of the whole complex that contained everything the emperor had in his life or could need in the life after death. … The statues have been painted after firing. … The priming layer consists of East Asian lacquer, a natural product that is obtained by injuring the bark of the lacquer tree and collecting the sap. It turns black during the hardening process. It is—and always has been—very precious, so priming the terracotta statues with … lacquer is a luxury."

One tourist who recently visited the museum praised the facility and its contents: "I was very impressed with the preservation that had gone on here and upon closer inspection with a good zoom lens, you could imagine these warriors had died only yesterday. You can even see individual facial expressions and hairstyles on these life-sized warriors. You should realize that the members of the Terracotta Army are dressed in accordance to their rank (and this includes their hairstyles), with the generals being the tallest. Originally, these warriors also carried weapons, such as swords, but most of these were thought to have been looted soon after burial. …Pit 1 is clearly the largest and the most impressive, as it has 11 rows of warriors, each dug 7 feet down into the ground and about 10 feet wide. Pit 1 includes most of the actual low-ranked warriors themselves, whereas Pit 2 has the cavalry and infantry units (complete with horses), and Pit 3 includes high-ranking officers and some war chariots. Many of the warriors from the Terracotta Army have been damaged, and while it is fair to assume this has occurred naturally over time (they have been buried for centuries, after all), I actually learned that this damaged occurred during the looting of weapons. There is on-going restoration to try to return these damaged warriors to something close to their original state."

Given that people's fascination with the Terracotta Army remains strong in the 21st century and the figures are still being constantly worked on by a modern army of scientists, it seems that Emperor Qin Shi Huang finally got his wish for immortality.

Bibliography

Clements, Jonathan (2007). *The First Emperor of China*. Sutton.

Debainne-Francfort, Corrine (1999). *The Search for Ancient China*. Discoveries. New York: Harry N. Abrams.

Dillon, Michael (1998). *China: A Historical and Cultural Dictionary*. Durham East Asia series. Richmond, Surrey: Curzon.

Portal, Jane (2007). *The First Emperor: China's Terracotta Army*. Harvard University Press.

Perkins, Dorothy (1999). *Encyclopedia of China: The Essential Reference to China, Its History and Culture*. New York: Facts on File.

Made in the USA
San Bernardino, CA
20 December 2019

61988472R00029